The Harlem Renaissance: The History and Legacy of Early 20th Century America's Most Influential Cultural Movement

By Charles River Editors

A picture of three women in Harlem in the 1920s

About Charles River Editors

Charles River Editors is a boutique digital publishing company, specializing in bringing history back to life with educational and engaging books on a wide range of topics. Keep up to date with our new and free offerings with this 5 second sign up on our weekly mailing list, and visit Our Kindle Author Page to see other recently published Kindle titles.

We make these books for you and always want to know our readers' opinions, so we encourage you to leave reviews and look forward to publishing new and exciting titles each week.

Introduction

"*An' the stars began to fall.*"

By Douglas

"An' the stars began to fall" by Aaron Douglas

The Harlem Renaissance

"Sometimes, I feel discriminated against, but it does not make me angry. It merely astonishes me. How can any deny themselves the pleasure of my company? It's beyond me." - Zora Neale Hurston

The Great Migration was the name coined for the mass movement of African-Americans north of the Mason-Dixon line in the years following the Civil War and the abolition of slavery. The enormous promise of emancipation proved to be illusory for the majority of Southern blacks, whether free or formerly enslaved, and as a result, hundreds of thousand made use of their fundamental freedom to leave.

This resulted in a "push" away from the South, caused by ongoing discrimination, entrenched Jim Crow laws, and increasing violence directed at blacks by whites. This was largely a movement driven by unreconciled whites who were apt to remind blacks that while slavery might have ended, equality should not be expected in its place.[1] At the same time, another aspect was the "pull" towards seemingly greater opportunities available in the North. There were many reasons for this, but mainly it had to do with the massive industrial stimulus brought about by World War I. While the United States may not have been directly engaged in the war, the nation's industrial resources certainly were.

Initially, the jobs created by this surge in industrialization were not available to blacks because of union restrictions intended to protect white labor, but

---

[1] *Jim Crow Laws* were state and local laws that enforced racial segregation in the Southern United States. "Jim Crow" was a folk character depicting a pejorative stereotype of a black man.

when the war broke out in Europe in 1914, this changed dramatically. European immigration to the United States evaporated almost overnight, creating an immediate labor vacuum in the United States, and although this did not mollify restive white labor unions, it nonetheless created a surge in opportunities for blacks.

Generally, the Great Migration is defined as having occurred between 1916 and 1970, during which time some 6 million African-Americans left the South for various northern states, not only primarily in the Northeast, but also in large numbers to the Midwest and the West. The First Great Migration, which took place mainly between 1916 and 1930, would bring about the Harlem Renaissance. The Second Great Migration, of course, occurred due to a similar industrialization that took place between 1940 and 1970. The figure typically cited for the First Great Migration is 1.6 million, and the phenomenon was ended temporarily mainly by the Great Depression, which reduced opportunities in the North considerably and made rural lifestyles more preferable for a time.

The main centers of black migration during the first wave were not only the industrial cities in the Northeast, mainly New York and Philadelphia, but also Detroit, Pittsburgh, St. Louis, Cleveland and Chicago, among others. Indeed, the African-American population in New York in particular exploded during this period, from about

140,000 in 1910 to upwards of 650,000 by 1940. In Philadelphia, during the same period, the black population increased by almost 230,000, and Chicago had an even bigger increase.

This migration, multi-faceted and multi-directional, found its principal cultural focus in New York City, most notably in Harlem. While many of these opportunities were made possible thanks to the work of Philip Payton, Jr., a prominent black businessman and real estate developer, no two historians will agree on the exact origins of the Harlem Renaissance, and there are few that are able to categorically agree on what the phenomenon actually represented. What is inescapable, however, is that a black cultural movement coalesced spontaneously in that area of uptown Manhattan.

The Harlem Renaissance: The History and Legacy of Early 20th Century America's Most Influential Cultural Movement examines the events and works that occurred in and around Harlem, and how they affected the world at large. Along with pictures and a bibliography, you will learn about the Harlem Renaissance like never before.

The Great Migration

"We have a right, in our effort to get just treatment, to insist that we produce something of the best in human character and that it is unfair to judge us by our criminals and prostitutes." – W.E.B. Du Bois

At the turn of the 20th century, Harlem was a predominately white neighborhood in Manhattan, but it was here that a loosely configured organic movement began. Incoming blacks, arriving in New York from many quarters, began to drift into Manhattan, occupying cheap rooms and apartments across the neighborhood until its character became more noticeably black. This caught the attention of an aspiring young black entrepreneur by the name of Philip Payton, Jr. As the story goes, Payton, Jr. entered the family barbering business while his two brothers attended Yale University. Frustrated at the lack of investment in his education, Payton tried various jobs, eventually finding himself employed as a janitor in a real estate firm. This led to a few private ventures into real estate and property management, and although not always successful, his progress was steady. His first newspaper advertisement read, "Colored man makes a speciality of managing colored tenements."

Payton, Jr.

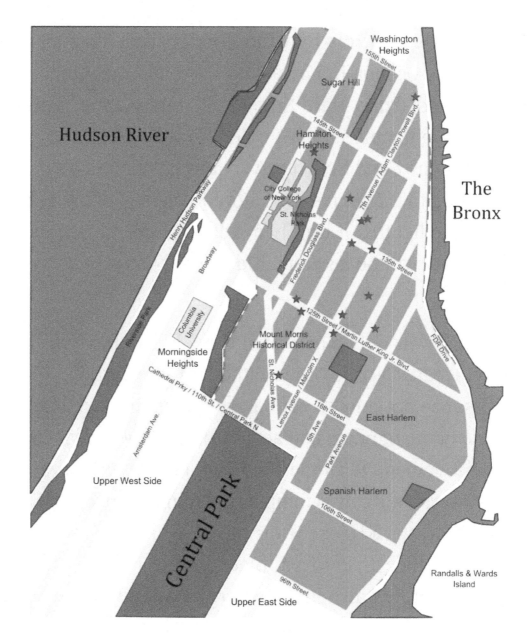

A map of Harlem

Initially, these changes met with considerable local resistance. In 1905, the *New York Herald* ran a headline that declared, "Negros Move into Harlem." The story continued, "An untoward circumstance has been injected into the private dwelling market in the vicinity of 133rd and 134th Streets. During the last three years flats that were occupied entirely by white folks…have been captured for occupation by a Negro population. One Hundred and Thirty-third Street still shows some signs of resistance to the blending of colors in that street, but between Lenox and Seventh Avenues has practically succumbed to the ingress of colored tenants…Real estate brokers predict that it is only a matter of time when the entire block will be a stronghold of the Negro population."

Indeed, it was only a matter of time. Philip Payton, Jr. owes his status as one of the fathers of the Harlem Renaissance not only to his business acumen, but also because he recognized and acted upon the potential for a social movement. On June 15, 1904, he chartered the Afro-American Realty Company. An initial offer of 50,000 shares at $10 each was made, which attracted small-scale investment from black investors interested not only in profit, but also in the emerging mood of black cohesion, empowerment, and organization. The concept of housing appealed to a grassroots urge for social justice on behalf of blacks, and a developing sense within the new dispensation that anything was possible.

His prospectus, published in support of the first share issue, was overtly political, appealing to black investors as black investors. It told readers, "Now is the time to buy. If you want to be numbered among those of the race who are doing something towards solving the so-called 'Race Problem.'" This was powerful, and it was successful, but while Payton, Jr. may have had a strong sense of racial destiny, he was not beyond using the realpolitik of race in the United States to his advantage.

In 1905, the white-owned Hudson Realty Company purchased a tract of land on West 135th Street, near Lenox Avenue. This land was in the heart of Harlem, and the company aimed to construct a residential development. In order to make the development more attractive to prospective investors, the Company also acquired three neighboring tenement buildings from Afro-American Realty. To the dismay of Payton, Jr.'s investors, however, and entirely in contravention of the social policies of Afro-American Realty, the Hudson Realty Company evicted all black tenants and replaced them with whites. In addition, Hudson's builders and developers agreed only to rent their future properties to whites.

The Afro-American Realty Company responded by acquiring two adjacent apartment houses, evicting their white tenants and replacing them with the blacks evicted by Hudson. This resulted in a sudden and precipitous collapse of property values, and eventually the Hudson Company was forced to sell the original three buildings back to Afro-American Realty at a significant loss.

This was a shrewd business maneuver, but it was also a political coup, and it enhanced Payton, Jr.'s reputation as a businessman, which attracted even more investment in his company. In a fit of pique, the *New York Times* called Payton, Jr.'s move a "Real Estate Race War," which is precisely what it was.

The Afro-American Realty Company began thereafter to aggressively acquire, by purchase or lease, houses, tenements and apartment buildings, especially in and around Harlem. Blacks from neighboring districts began to move into Harlem, and by the time the Great Migration began to gather momentum after 1910, Harlem had developed a conspicuously black complexion.

Black migration into New York at this time was not solely limited to the movement north of disenfranchised blacks from the Southern states. In fact, it included also a steady inflow from the Caribbean, and black immigrants from Jamaica, Haiti, Puerto Rico, and the Dominicans added a unique cultural and social diversity to the growing population. Perhaps the best known Caribbean immigrant of the 20th century was the Jamaican-born Marcus Garvey, who would influence the movement with a mood of militant black nationalism, infusing the parallel literary and artistic movement with an aggressive and militant edge. Thus, by the end of the first decade of the 20th century, the stage was set for an energetic rediscovery and merger of black political, literary and artistic expression, all bundled together in a phenomenon that came to be known as the Harlem Renaissance.

Garvey

The Politics of Revival

"History is the landmark by which we are directed into the true course of life. The history of a movement, the history of a nation, the history of a race is the guide-post of that movement's destiny, that nation's destiny, that race's destiny. What you do today that is worthwhile, inspires others to act at some future time." – Marcus Garvey

The journey from slavery to emancipation was one of multiple stages, and its steps can be plotted either by the creation or the repeal of laws. The most famous of these was the Thirteenth Amendment to the Constitution, adopted on December 18, 1865, abolishing slavery and enforced servitude. This was followed by the Fourteenth Amendment, adopted on July 9, 1868, addressing citizenship rights and equal protection under the law. Between 1870 and 1871, these two amendments were reinforced by three bills debated and passed by Congress known as the Enforcement Acts. The Enforcement Acts were criminal codes specifically protecting African-Americans' rights to vote, hold office, serve on juries, and be guaranteed equal protection under laws. They also allowed the federal government to intervene when states did not act to protect these rights.

The principal goal of the Enforcement Acts was to

improve conditions for blacks during the Reconstruction period, mainly by targeting the Ku Klux Klan and other racist organizations that emerged in the aftermath of emancipation. The purpose of these, of course, was to pursue an agenda of discrimination, and to intimidate blacks in areas where freedoms were guaranteed by law. Most importantly, the Enforcement Acts were intended to prohibit the use of violence, coercion or any type of intimidation to limit or deny black freedom of access to suffrage rights.

Ultimately, the effects of these federal laws and Constitutional amendments were nullified considerably by a lack of will to enforce them. In addition to that, white, Democratic-dominated legislatures in the South began introducing what came to be known as Jim Crow laws. Purporting to be pragmatic in a highly prejudicial race environment, these laws and conventions utilized the phrase "Separate but Equal" in regards to the status of blacks in every aspect of daily life, from public transportation to public education. Jim Crow was solidified by a number of Supreme Court challenges to the Civil Rights Act of 1875, which resulted in the invalidation of the Act in 1883 on the grounds that it addressed social rights, not civil rights. The Court noted that the Fourteenth Amendment protected people against violations of their civil rights by states, not by the actions of individuals. This cleared the way for individual state legislatures to enact laws that legalized racial segregation in practically all public places, from schools to hospitals, cinemas, theaters, and restaurants. In 1896, the Supreme Court's decision in *Plessy v. Ferguson* upheld these laws, establishing the infamous doctrine of separate and equal by concluding that segregation did not violate the equal protection clause of the Fourteenth Amendment so long as the facilities for blacks and whites were equal.

Separation was established under these laws, but equality certainly was not. Facilities made available to blacks were inevitably inferior and underfunded, and the practical effects of the Jim Crow laws were the reestablishment of institutionalized racism and discrimination across the South.

Meanwhile, racism in the North, while not statutory to the same extent, was nonetheless a matter of fact thanks to understood conventions of housing segregation, banking lending practices, and job discrimination. The U.S. military was already segregated, but at the request of Southern cabinet members, and in response to Postmaster General Albert Burleson's plan to segregate the Railway Mail Service, President Woodrow Wilson introduced federal workplace segregation in 1913, reflecting many of the practices already established in the South.

Wilson

Burleson

This was the broad social landscape facing blacks in the United States at the turn of the 20th century, and while the cities of the North became the origins of black cultural rediscovery, its early manifestation was very much within the separate but equal doctrine, with "separate" tending to dominate.

There are two early voices that stand out as pioneers and standard bearers in the early movement of black revival associated with the Harlem Renaissance. William Edward Burghardt Du Bois was born in Great Barrington,

Massachusetts in 1868, under extremely humble circumstances. His father Alfred abandoned the family early, and his mother supported the family as a domestic servant. He thrived in the public school system, however, revealing a commanding intellect, a vivid imagination, and a powerful sense of his own destiny. His higher education began at Fisk University, a private, historically black university in Nashville, Tennessee. Here he gained both a classical education and his first exposure to life in the South under the regime of the Jim Crow laws. From Fisk, he headed to Harvard, graduating in 1895 with a doctorate in history. His Ph.D. dissertation, *The Suppression of the African Slave Trade to the United States of America*, was published a year later in book form, the first of what would be more than two dozen books accredited to him.

Du Bois

From Harvard, Du Bois spent two years at the University of Berlin, studying sociology and establishing the bedrock of intellectual activism that would form his future political identity. He believed then, as he would continue to believe, that each race possessed its own peculiar gifts, and that within a cosmopolitan world there could exist a "kingdom of culture," both individual and collective, beyond the constraining race conventions of the United States.

Back in the United States, he found himself limited when

it came to choosing institutions in which to pursue an academic career, so he drifted until, as a member of the faculty of Atlanta University, he completed and published what is widely regarded as his literary masterwork. *The Souls of Black Folk* is a collection of essays, snippets of autobiography and fiction, intended, as he described it, to illuminate the subjective human reality of those who lived "within the veil." Although he intended his audience to be white, *The Souls of Black Folk* would prove in the end to have a far greater impact on black readers, and in particular the artists, poets and writers who formed the bedrock of the Harlem Renaissance.

It also began to more clearly define Du Bois himself, and where he stood in the emerging black movement. In this regard, he is perhaps best defined by his at first respectful, but then increasingly acrimonious opposition to the work and ideas of Booker T. Washington. Washington, 12 years Du Bois' senior and born into slavery, entered the field of education and founded the famous Tuskegee Institute based on his vision of what a population emerging from generations of slavery required in order to successfully integrate into modern life. His position was simply one of incremental entry by the provision of industrial education and political accommodation. He urged blacks to accept discrimination in the short term and concentrate on elevating themselves, thereby proving themselves through hard work and material prosperity.

Washington

Du Bois would have none of that, believing it amounted to an approval of the Jim Crow regime of the South and a passive acceptance of racism. In opposition, he and other black leaders organized the Niagara Movement, citing opposition to Washington's moral leadership of the movement and marking their determination to fight for full civil equality for black Americans.[2] The movement

[2] The *Niagara Movement* was founded in 1905 as a black civil rights organization. It was led by W. E. B. Du Bois and William Monroe Trotter, and so-named for the "mighty current" of change the group wished to promote. Niagara Falls was the setting

did not gain much traction, but it was in direct line of ascension to the much more influential National Association for the Advancement of Colored People (NAACP).

In 1910, Du Bois moved to New York City to take office as the director of publicity for the NAACP, and to edit its monthly journal, *The Crisis*. Du Bois did not find much common ground with the predominately white leadership of the NAACP, but through the predominately black readership of *The Crisis*, his name became widely known. In many respects, his views on such themes as lynching, America's entry into World War I, Bolshevism, pan-Africanism, Garveyism, and the New Deal became the themes for racial politics throughout the period. No debate or discussion in the field of black politics in the United States during this period could justly be regarded as complete until Du Bois had made his contribution.

Inevitably, Du Bois began to position himself as a patron and pathfinder of the new literary and artistic movement forming around the Harlem Renaissance. Long before the likes of Alain Locke and James Weldon Johnson, it was Du Bois who recognized that artistic and literary creation, far more than a crude acceptance of industrial education and discrimination, would prove black legitimacy in a

of the first meeting that called for opposition to racial segregation and disenfranchisement, and opposition to policies of accommodation and conciliation promoted by African-American leaders such as Booker T. Washington.

world of white creation. He insisted that the black man was the original American artist, that the "rude melodies" of black slaves were the only authentic American music, and that it was only black laughter, dance, and song that gave meaning to an otherwise empty, materialistic American culture.

James Weldon Johnson

To this he added practical impetus. Through *The Crisis*, he launched a competition for black writers, and in 1921 unearthed the genius of, among others, Langston Hughes, through his epochal poem "The Negro Speaks of Rivers." In the end, however, Du Bois is generally regarded to have been guilty of artistic and intellectual snobbery, and his inability to climb down from Wagner and Beethoven to embrace Louis Armstrong and Billie Holliday, or

Byron and Tennyson for Langton Hughes and Claude McKay, tended to compound his estrangement from the very movement that he was instrumental in creating.

Hughes

From about the mid-1920s to the onset of the Great Depression, Du Bois existed somewhat on the fringes of the movement, attempting to inject gravitas with his continued appeals to the great classical forms and his calls to blacks to compete, not simply mimic. He might have gained some satisfaction as the 1930s dawned and it seemed his vision held more longevity than those who he once criticized. Once the "New Negro" movement had passed beyond the vitality of the Harlem Renaissance and into the longer struggle for cultural and social emancipation, it has tended to be Du Bois' particular message that is probably best remembered as scholars reflect back on the struggle of the 1920s.

If Booker T. Washington preached a vision of patience and incremental growth in a world of white predominance and Du Bois challenged the bastions of white cultural and intellectual superiority, it was Marcus Garvey who epitomized a new political assertiveness in a world of black industrial labor. Often regarded as the "Negro Moses," Garvey was the progenitor of Black Pride and Modern Black Nationalism, and, as such, his influence projects far beyond the Harlem Renaissance. Despite the failure of many of lofty and quixotic schemes, his signature contribution to the New Negro Movement was the moral uplifting he offered to a people inculcated with a sense of their own inferiority. Freedom from material bondage was one thing, but Garvey was among those who freed people from psychological bondage, and in many respects that would be the defining triumph of the Harlem Renaissance as a whole.

Born on August 17, 1887 in the tiny seaside town of St. Ann's Bay on the north coast of Jamaica, Garvey enjoyed none of Du Bois' academic accomplishments, but as Du Bois contended with his own bourgeois tendencies, Garvey was effortlessly a man of the people. He was a printer by trade, a self-taught elocutionist and public speaker, and the publisher of several small newspapers. As was true for many young blacks from the Caribbean, his first political education was acquired through unions and labor organization, in this case on the sugar plantations of his home island.

In 1910, he left Jamaica and spent several years traveling through South and Central America, and his political ideology evolved as a synthesis of many influences, not only with touches of Du Bois' pan-Africanism and Booker T. Washington's pragmatism, but also with the aspirations and expectations of a black society moving beyond the conventions of plantations and colonial authority. From 1912-1914, he traveled around Europe, taking classes in law and philosophy in Birkbeck College at the University of London, while at the same time contributing to the *African Times and Orient Review*, published by Dusé Mohamed Ali. Dusé Mohamed Ali was an Egyptian-Sudanese intellectual and activist who was known for his radical positions on African Nationalism, and who exerted a considerable influence on a generation of politically alert Africans and black diasporians. He had a considerable influence on Garvey, who could frequently be found speaking at Hyde Park's Speakers' Corner.

Upon returning to Jamaica, Garvey was initially inclined to follow in the ideological footsteps of Booker T.

Washington, preaching accommodation with colonial rule, eschewing politics, and urging a one-step-at-a-time approach to black education and advancement. This, one can suppose, was a pragmatic position, probably based on the fact that accommodation with British standards of race relations was easier than those in the United States at the time.

His first visit to the United States in 1916, however, began to quickly change his mind. By then, Booker T. Washington had been dead for about a year and the "New Negro" era was finding its feet. Visiting the Tuskegee Institute was something of a pilgrimage, but the reality was that in the South, Garvey encountered racism on a scale he had never before experienced. The United States was a potboiler of race politics far beyond his experience, and the style of his activism was altered dramatically as a consequence.

In 1917, the city of East St. Louis erupted into bloody race riots. The cause and effect of the East St Louis riots are complex and multifaceted, but in its simplest terms, the influx of black workers into traditionally white-dominated industries generated tensions, exacerbated by cultural differences and racism. The reaction of white labor and white labor organizations was a violent anti-black purge, either ignored or supported by the police.

Garvey was galvanized by this event, and in response he founded an American chapter of the Universal Negro Improvement Association (UNIA). On July 8, 1917, on behalf of the Association, he delivered a lengthy speech at the Lafayette Hall, addressing an enthusiastic audience of local and Caribbean blacks. In the speech, he thundered, "The East St Louis Riot, or rather massacre…will go down in history as one of the bloodiest outrages of against mankind for which any class of people could be held guilty. This is no time for fine words, but a time to lift one's voice against the savagery of a people who claim to be the dispensers of democracy."

This was Garvey's political coming of age, and within a few years he would emerge as one of the most influential and compelling black leaders of the generation. An electrifying speaker, he was able to present and develop a message of economic and cultural independence that has since come to be known as "Garveyism." Garveyism could probably be best described as the liberation of Africa from colonial rule and the spiritual redemption of the black race. Garvey saw Africa as a fallen society estranged from a past greatness that had to be restored in order for Africa to take its rightful place in the world. Key to this redemption was the fact that it could only be achieved by the black races themselves.

During this period, a significant interaction was

beginning to occur between Africans and African-Americans as an increasing number of young blacks from Africa arrived in the United States to gain access to higher education. This was occurring often under the aegis of various independent churches beginning to appear throughout colonial Africa. The bedrock of the movement was known as "Ethiopianism," inspired by the Biblical passage found in Psalm 68:31: "Ethiopia shall soon stretch forth its hands unto God." This phrase was liberally interpreted by numerous breakaway churches in Africa to imply a direct communication between the black race and God for the divine purpose of the emancipation of the people. Traditional, white-dominated missionary churches, which had in many cases pioneered colonial occupation and introduced Christianity to the continent, were seen as inimical to black progress. The independent churches did not necessarily turn their backs on the essential elements of the Christian faith, but they certainly populated it with black ideals and used its institutions as an early template for political organization.

One of the earliest and most powerful trans-Atlantic ecumenical affiliations was the African Methodist Episcopal Church, the first independent black church in the United States. It inspired numerous similar chapters in South Africa and elsewhere, and the AME remains one of the largest black churches in South Africa today.

Garvey, it must be said, did not function within the church - he remained strictly secular - but his movement of black redemption, alongside Du Bois' pan-Africanism, dovetailed into one another within an explosion of self-awareness that was taking place across the black diaspora. The main vehicle of Garveyism was the Universal Negro Improvement Association (UNIA), the dynamic core of which was Harlem. The six-block radius encompassing 135th Street and Lenox Avenue was home to the UNIA's international headquarters, as well as the spiritual home of the movement, Liberty Hall. It was also where the offices of all major UNIA affiliated enterprises were located.

The best known of these was the Black Star Line, a shipping line incorporated by Garvey and other members of UNIA. The Black Star Line was intended to perform as a vehicle to spread black people and black business throughout the global economy, and eventually to facilitate the return of American blacks to Africa in a mass migration informally known as the Back-to-Africa movement. The Black Star Line probably had a greater cultural than economic impact; despite a promising start, and strong capitalization, it only operated between 1919 and 1922. Other UNIA enterprises included the Universal Printing House, Negro Factories Corporation, and the widely distributed and highly successful *Negro World* weekly newspaper.

Garvey, in practical terms, was a quixotic and rather eccentric character who was not only adored at the grassroots level of the movement but also seen often as an embarrassment by the black intelligentsia and other leaders. He based himself in Harlem in the early 1920s, and he was frequently seen parading in the uniform and cocked hat of an imperial viceroy. Du Bois, never one for levity, described Marcus Garvey as "without doubt, the most dangerous enemy of the Negro race in America and in the world. He is either a lunatic or a traitor." His main objection was to Garvey's elemental assertion that no black person could hope to obtain American citizenship, and that forcible separation and removal of all blacks to Africa was the only solution to the "Negro Problem." Ironically, Du Bois eventually died in Ghana after renouncing his American citizenship.

For his part, Garvey in turn accused Du Bois of prejudice based on his own lighter skin and academic pedigree. Du Bois referred to Garvey as an ugly, fat black man, and Garvey called Du Bois "a white man's n*****."

It was, therefore, with some relief to Du Bois that Garvey's deportation was eventually engineered by the federal government. In 1927, he was sent back to Jamaica.

Art

"You are young, gifted and black. We must begin to tell

our young, there's a world waiting for you, yours is the quest that has just begun." - James Weldon Johnson

The Harlem Renaissance was primarily an artistic movement, in part to rediscover and establish black cultural autonomy, but also in part to stand as proof of a black coming of age in modern America. The latter theme tended to be championed by the likes of Du Bois, who saw the acme of black achievement as parallel to the acme of white achievement. As he put it, "It is unfair to judge us by our criminals and prostitutes." In his view of the movement, if the pinnacle of black expression could equal the pinnacle of white expression, then blacks had a fair claim to equality with whites.

There were many who conformed to this view, both rhetorically and in terms of their literary and artistic output, but there were many who did not. Aaron Douglas was one of the leading black visual artists of the age, and his view of the objective of black American art was strikingly different than Du Bois' views. He wrote, "Our problem is to conceive, develop, establish an art era. Not white art painting black…let's bare our arms and plunge them deep through laughter, through pain, through sorrow, through hope, through disappointment, into the very depths of the souls of our people and drag forth material crude, rough, neglected. Then let's sing it, dance it, write it, paint it. Let's do the impossible. Let's create something transcendentally material, mystically objective. Earthy. Spiritually earthy. Dynamic."

Douglas

Aaron Douglas' influence on the Harlem Renaissance is visible almost everywhere. He was an illustrator and muralist, and he was only by happenstance part of the Harlem Renaissance scene. Passing through New York in 1925 en route to Paris to augment his bachelor's degree from the University of Nebraska, he was persuaded by what he saw taking place in Harlem to stay. His first major commission was to illustrate Alain Locke's book *The New Negro*, which led to a flurry of magazine illustrations and appearances in numerous high profile books, including those of writers such as Langston Hughes, Charles S. Johnson, Countee Cullen, Claude McKay, Wallace Thurman, and James Weldon Johnson. His work typified the synthesis of established, modernist forms with the stylized and geometric patterns and shapes of African art. It was characterized by the use of art deco silhouettes, enhanced by the rhythmic incorporation of circles, diagonals and wavy lines. Perhaps more acutely than any other black artist during this period, it was Douglas who quantified the aspirations of the "New Negro" by forging an original path for black political and creative freedom.

Sharon Mollerus' picture of Aaron Douglas'
Aspiration

Although Douglas based himself in Harlem, the most notable black artists of the period based themselves in Paris, where they found a greater appreciation and a wider appeal. This had much to do with a parallel movement in Paris at the time that is nowadays referred to as the Paris Noir, or Black Paris. Artistic audiences in France at the time, especially in Paris, were more accepting and understanding of black art, and black artists from the United States found an environment within which they could create art with more freedom.

The Paris scene with regards to black music and performance is discussed further below, but it was in part the forging of a black American presence in Paris by early jazz and ragtime musicians that created the artistic space for the sculptors, painters, writers, and poets who followed. The French's overseas empire was at its peak in the early 20th century, and France's relationship with African colonies was tending to establish a better appreciation of the indigenous African art that was beginning to find its way into galleries and private collections throughout the country.

The Great Depression, however, forced many black artists to return to the United States, which meant, ironically, that most of the best work in the visual arts associated with the Harlem Renaissance and the New Negro movement emerged in the 1930s. However, at the same time, exposure to the more liberal environment of Paris and its vibrant cultural atmosphere lent a great deal of individuality and sophistication to the work of black artists. In turn, this served to improve and sophisticate the work of local artists back in New York.

One of these artists was Palmer Hayden, a Columbia trained artist who depicted the African-American social landscape, working stylistically in both oils and watercolours. He studied at the Cooper Union in New York and independently at the Boothbay Art Colony in

Maine. In 1925, he created his first masterwork, "Fetiche et Fleurs," for which he was awarded the Harmon Foundation's Gold Award. This afforded him the patronage to live and study in France for five years.

Hayden

Another was Archibald J. Motley, described as a Jazz Age Modernist, who also spent time in France and painted vibrant scenes of black nightlife reflecting that period. He was classically trained at the Art Institute of Chicago, which is revealed more frequently in his portraiture. His artistic roots, however, tended to remain in Chicago, and while he is listed as one of the major contributors to the Harlem Renaissance, he was also instrumental in a parallel movement known informally as the Chicago Renaissance.

Motley's self-portrait

Palmer Hayden and Archibald Motley were both modernists and entirely true to African-American subject matter and the black experience, but a more classic strain of expression was evident in the works of one of the signature artists of the New Negro Movement, Sargent Claude Johnson. Johnson's carvings, ceramics, and paintings reflected a deeper interest in African forms of art, and Johnson was arguably one of the foremost Harlem Renaissance artists, producing in a style that would have certainly made Du Bois proud. Johnson's works ranged from sculptures to carvings, masks, murals and paintings, and while they covered a spectrum of forms, the African themes are unmistakable. Perhaps lacking the specifics of a direct African identity, his works touched on numerous traditional African styles at the same time, with an identifiable loyalty to classic formality.

Johnson

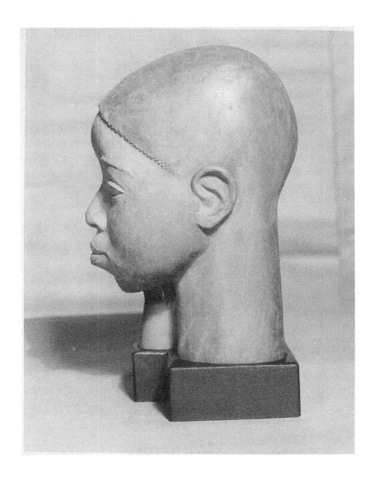

Johnson's "Chester," a portrait of a young African boy

Perhaps the finest sculptor of the movement, and of the era altogether, was Augusta Savage. She wished to be remembered not as a black or a female artist, but simply as an artist, and she was an academic art advocate, traveler, and pioneer in the evolution of American art. Much of her work was influenced by Africa as much as America, but at all times it displayed evidence of profound talent and exceptional training. She was one of the longest living artists of the Harlem Renaissance, and she is now considered a major figure of the Civil Rights

Movement.

Savage

Augusta Savage and her sculpture *Realization*

Augusta Savage was another who worked in an accomplished, classical style, producing bronze busts of many prominent African-American leaders, including Du Bois. In 1922, she was granted a scholarship to study in France, but the scholarship was removed when white students from Alabama who had received similar scholarships refused to travel unless hers was rescinded. Her appeal against the prohibition was unsuccessful, but it prompted a lifelong interest in the development and advocacy of young black artists, which perhaps, in the end, won her greater recognition than her art. Her celebrated bust of a Harlem child, Gamin (1929), made her name as an artist, and it secured her a scholarship to study at the Academie de la Grande Chaumiere in Paris. In France, she was associated with other black American expatriates Henry Ossawa Tanner, Claude McKay, and Countee Cullen.

Another great artist during the period was Meta Vaux Warrick Fuller, a poet, painter, and sculptor whose classical European influence is perhaps more noticeable. Her work, nonetheless, was distinctly Afrocentric, and she was described by the French press as "the delicate sculptor of horrors." Celebrated French sculptor Auguste Rodin described her as "one of the most imaginative Black artists of her generation." She is generally accepted, alongside Augusta Savage, as one of the first African-American female sculptors of importance, and a prominent member of the Harlem Renaissance. More than any other, her work symbolized the new "black identity" emerging as a consequence of the Harlem Renaissance, representing a new pride in African and black heritage and identity.

Fuller

Fuller's *Ethiopia Awakening*

Literature

"My soul has grown deep like the rivers." – Langston Hughes, "The Negro Speaks of Rivers" (1920)

The output of poetry and literature produced by the New Negro Movement probably surpasses the visual arts, and it was certainly through the written word that the movement is best appreciated and understood. The literature of the period did not simply take the form of published works of prose or poetry, but also the establishment of influential periodicals and journals, journalism, and drama. By the

1920s, many of these works and expressions had begun to achieve critical appreciation and popular acclaim in both white and black circles. While some remained true to traditional English literary forms, others utilized black vernacular speech and lyrical forms that appealed and identified with the black public.

For those who regard the Harlem Renaissance as primarily a literary movement, its emergence can be traced to a seminal event that took place on March 21, 1924. The event was conceived by Charles S. Johnson, the editor of the academic journal *Opportunity: A Journal of Negro Life*, published by the National Urban League to mark the publication of Jessie Fauset's first novel, *There Is Confusion*.[3]

---

[3] The *National Urban League* (NUL), *formerly known as the National League on Urban Conditions Among Negroes*, was founded in New York City on September 29, 1910, and is a nonpartisan civil rights organization advocating on behalf of African-Americans and against racial discrimination in the United States.

Johnson

Fauset, an editor, poet, essayist, novelist, and educator, was arguably among the most influential African-American writers emerging at the time, and the publication of *There Is Confusion* marked a watershed moment in the stereotypical portrayal of African-Americans in literature, particularly African-American women. It implied a newfound confidence that seemed to set Fauset's fictional characters apart from other characterizations of the time, as well as setting Fauset apart from other writers of her era.

At the time, *Opportunity* had been in publication for a

little over a year, during which Johnson, among others, had been building black American literature as a vehicle to express black cultural maturity and equality. The publication of *There Is Confusion* presented the opportunity to stage an event that would mark the emergence of a truly accomplished black writer. The venue chosen was the Civic Club, located near 12th St. and 5th Ave., about 100 blocks south of Harlem. Johnson initially planned a small reception that would include a handful of white publishers, editors, and literary critics, along with black intellectuals and young black writers. However, when he asked Alain Locke to preside over the event, Locke would agree only if the dinner was expanded to include African-American writers in general rather than a single novelist.

Alain Locke, another seminal figure of the Harlem Renaissance, was born on September 13, 1885, in Philadelphia, Locke is usually described as a philosopher, scholar, educator, and journalist, but these labels hardly suffice. He was one of the founding writers and literary giants of the Harlem Renaissance, with an academic career spanning Harvard and Oxford University in Britain, where he was the first black man to be awarded a Rhodes Scholarship. His most influential work was *The New Negro*, published in 1925 and providing a name for the movement that defined the concept of a renewed black vision for the 20th century. He was tacitly homosexual, and he added a certain amount of understated advocacy to other young black homosexuals in New York at the time, but he maintained a limited profile in an environment that was almost universally intolerant of gays.

Locke

In the end, the Civic Club Dinner grew into a gala occasion that hosted over 100 guests, including Du Bois, James Weldon Johnson, and numerous representatives of the new black intelligentsia. Jessie Fauset headed an assembly of black poets and writers. The whites present were predominantly publishers and literary critics, headed by the editor of *Century* magazine Carl Van Doren, who called upon the young writers in the audience to make their contribution to the "new literary age" evolving in America.[4]

The Civic Club Dinner created a bridge between African-American intellectuals and writers, and together they would rapidly accelerate the literary phase of the Harlem Renaissance. In a single movement, they liberated black literary expression from its shackles of tradition. According to author David Levering Lewis in his 1981 book *When Harlem Was in Vogue*, "White capital and influence were crucial, and the white presence, at least in the early years, hovered over the New Negro world of art and literature like a benevolent censor, politely but persuasively setting the outer limits of its creative boundaries."

Music

"If you have to ask what jazz is, you'll never know." – Louis Armstrong

There is a tendency in the popular imagination to picture the music of the Harlem Renaissance as jazz and little

---

[4] Van Doren, Carl. *The Younger Generation of Negro Writers*, Opportunity 2 (1924): 144–45.

more, but while the movement did produce an evolution in jazz music, the New Negro Movement offered up black talent and vitality into all branches of popular and modern music.

For those who consider the Harlem Renaissance to be a more musical movement, many agree that the Harlem Renaissance began with the 1921 staging at the famous 63rd Street Musical Hall of a musical revue called *Shuffle Along*. *Shuffle Along* was written by Vaudeville comedians Flournoy Miller and Aubrey Lyles, with a score composed by composers/singers Eubie Blake and Noble Sissle and a cast of largely unknown performers. Among the performers were Josephine Baker and Paul Robeson, both destined for international stardom. The significance of the production, at least in the words of Eubie Blake, was that it achieved what many other notable black performers had failed to do. "We did it, that's the story," he said. "We put Negroes back on Broadway!" [5]

---

[5] **Eubie Blake**, in *Harlem Speaks: A Living History of the Harlem Renaissance*, ed. Cary D. Wintz (Naperville, IL: Sourcebooks, 2007), 151–65.

The sheet music cover for *Shuffle Along*

Blake

Sissle

Many people see this event in a different light, and quite like the Civic Club Dinner, which few will deny marked the moment of recognition of black literature, the first performance of *Shuffle Along* defined the individual character of nightlife in Harlem. It certainly introduced white New York audiences to black music, theater and entertainment for the first time, helping create a fascination that would prove to be such a vital ingredient of the Harlem Renaissance. It also introduced jazz to Broadway, which was, in and of itself, a seminal moment. Jazz music and finely choreographed jazz dance routines created something entirely new and exciting on the stages of New York, and the show proved to be a critical and financial success, staging 474 shows on Broadway and numerous production companies. Before long, more black-written shows were appearing on Broadway, like *The Chocolate Dandies*. Furthermore, white writers and composers began to produce their own versions of black musical comedies.

Shuffle Along also opened the floodgates for the development of blues and jazz, and in combination with the experience of American musicians overseas, the concept of what is recognized as jazz today owes its roots very much to that sudden proliferation. Jazz was never a product of Harlem, nor of the New Negro Movement, but rather the evolution of musical forms with their roots in an earlier African-American experience, mainly in cities like New Orleans, Memphis, and St. Louis. From there, it moved along with the Great Migration, finding its classic forms in Chicago and New York before and during World War I.

According to James Weldon Johnson, jazz made its first appearance in New York in or around 1905, with the resident band at Proctor's Twenty-Third Street Theatre.

Johnson described the band as "a playing-singing-dancing orchestra, making dominant use of banjos, mandolins, guitars, saxophones, and drums in combination, and [it] was called the Memphis Students—a very good name, overlooking the fact that the performers were not students and were not from Memphis. There was also a violin, a couple of brass instruments, and a double-bass."[6]

One of the Memphis Students was James Reese Europe, who eventually became a prominent bandleader and composer. He performed with the Clef Club Orchestra at Carnegie Hall, and he subsequently joined the U.S. Expeditionary Force to Europe and helped introduce jazz to the French. In Harlem, jazz clubs began to spring up everywhere, and names like Ma Rainey and others began snapping up contracts, first with local black recording labels, and later with more prominent mainstream labels like Paramount and Columbia.

Iconic names such as the Alhambra Ballroom, the Apollo Theatre, Club Harlem, Lenox Lounge, Showman's Jazz Club and Minton's Playhouse and many others hosted the great names of the day, many of whom would become international stars. This included Ella Fitzgerald, Louis Armstrong, Count Basie, Billie Holliday, Cab Calloway, and many others.

---

[6] humanitiestexas.org

Négritude and the Paris Noir

"I have come back from France more firmly convinced than ever that Negros should write Negro music. We have our own racial feeling and if we try to copy whites we will make bad copies…we won France by playing music which was ours and not a pale imitation of others, and if we are to develop in America we must develop along our own lines." – James Reese Europe

The first decades of the 20th century marked a vibrant and productive period for the French colonies in Africa and the Caribbean. The French empire was at its peak, and Paris became the center of an emerging movement of black cultural awareness and revival. Although blacks within the French colonies were facing a similar (albeit much less extreme) form of racism than minorities in the United States, the same emphasis on reclaiming and securing black culture was underway. This was seen as a means of fighting back against the French belief that the obliteration of indigenous cultural expression and its replacement by a dominant French culture was ultimately in the best interests of both.

The evolution of black society in all of the African colonies was reaching a critical point. The last decade of the 19th century and the first few years of the 20th century had seen the fruition of black access to missionary-sponsored primary education. This helped to form the bedrock of a nominally educated class of black participants in the emerging colonial military, police, industrial, and administrative establishments. In turn, this formed the basis for the first generation of highly educated blacks, those of the 1930s and 1940s, who for the first time had access to overseas universities and who were returning to their respective colonies with academic degrees. This wholly revolutionized black society in both Africa and the Caribbean; it not only offered up a generation of young leaders conversant in modern politics and Western society, but also one determined to harness the potentialities of modern life in synthesis with their own cultures.

This was the essence of Négritude, and perhaps one of its greatest proponents was Leopold Senghor, a Senegalese intellectual and poet. Senegal was France's flagship territory in Africa, and the basis of the French interest in "assimilation." Assimilation was a moment in French colonial history when the concept of turning the black elite of the various colonies into black Frenchmen opened the institutions of France to direct participation from people in the colonies. In 1914, for example, the black ex-mayor of Dakar, Blaise Diagne, was elected to the French Chamber of Deputies as the representative of the main commune of Senegal, a high water mark in French relations with the colony.

By the time France had acquired control over most of West and Equatorial Africa, the concept of assimilating 60 million Africans was no longer practical. By then, however, a version of the Harlem Renaissance had already taken root in Paris. The influx of black intellectuals and aspirant leaders from all over Africa and the Caribbean, supported by numerous black American artists, intellectuals, writers and performers, created a vibrant black social and academic scene in the French capital.

Senghor arrived in Paris in 1928 at the age of 22, already educated to a high level at the French Lycee in Dakar. In Paris, he plunged into higher education, first at the Sorbonne and then the University of Paris, where he received the Agrégation in French Grammar. Later he was designated professor at the universities of Tours and Paris, teaching at both during the period of 1935–45. After World War II, he was selected as Dean of the Linguistics Department with the École nationale de la France d'Outre-Mer, a position he retained until 1960. In 1983, he was elected to the membership of the Académie Française, and he led Senegal to independence in 1960.

All of this demonstrated the opportunities that were available to young blacks during that crucial period corresponding with the New Negro Movement in the

United States, and what attracted so many black American participants in the Movement to Paris.

Négritude was not the sole creation of Leopold Senghor; in fact, he was perhaps one of the more conservative founders of the movement. Another was the young Martinican poet Aimé Césaire. Césaire was highly intellectual, and a classicist very much in the Du Bois pattern, but he was also fiercely loyal to his African roots and a great deal more hostile to French colonial practice than Senghor. Another was Léon Damas, a French Guianan poet and intellectual who also later became politically active in his colony. All three men met in Paris, and around them a clique of similarly minded black youth from the French colonial diaspora formed. Central to this clique were two Afro-Martiniquais sisters, Paulette and Jeanne Nardal, perhaps best described as intellectual socialites who provided a great deal of literary and social gravitas to the movement.

Paulette Nardal

Like Senghor and the other "fathers" of Négritude, the two Nardal sisters were born into the upper middle classes of their colony and gravitated to Paris to complete their higher education. Paulette Nardal was the first black person to study at the Sorbonne, followed a little later by her sister Jeanne. The two are credited with boosting the movement mainly through the social avenues provided by their salon, the Clamart Salon. Le Clamart Salon was a teashop venue in the Clamart district that was popular with the intelligentsia, and where Négritude philosophy was often discussed. However, both women, through their writing and journalism, and perhaps more importantly their refinement of the fundamental philosophy of

Négritude, helped to establish and solidify the movement. Paulette Nardal translated many of the works of the Harlem Renaissance writers into French, which provided a vital crossover between the two movements and helped to forge a common identity between them. Artists like Augusta Savage who were attempting to establish a place within the movement were aided significantly by the coverage they received from Paulette Nardal's writing and reporting. In October 1931, the sisters founded a journal called *La Revue du Monde Noir (Review of the Black World)*, which, although it only ran to six editions, became an extremely influential vehicle for expressing the pan-African ideal of Négritude. The final issue of *La Revue du Monde Noir* contained an essay written by Paulette Nardal entitled "Eveil de la conscience de race" ("The Awakening of Race Consciousness"), which, as the title implies, was a tour de force that defined the evolution of Afro-Caribbean race awareness.

The artistic and social liberty available in Paris was noticed first by black servicemen stationed in or passing through the city during World War I. Encountering for the first time an environment comparatively free of racism, many stayed, and others followed. By World War I, Paris already hosted a large black community, going back to the original Louisiana sale when upwards of 50,000 free blacks left North America to escape the threat of slavery, settling later in Paris. Of the 200,000 or so African-Americans on active service in France during World War I (alongside a similar number recruited from the colonies), quite a number stayed, at least for a while. Most were musicians, and they integrated easily into black Parisian society, providing a basis for others to follow in the 1920s and 1930s.

Even before this, an awareness of l'art negre, formed largely through the French colonial experience, was beginning to establish roots in Paris. Artists like Henri Matisse, André Derain, and Maurice de Vlaminck were already beginning to notice African art forms, and even Picasso, Braque, and Léger, as well as socialites and cultural promoters like Apollinaire and Jean Cocteau, were becoming aware of the African ideas and concepts now freely circulating around the capital.

With the American newcomers came jazz and the "Jazz Age," and the Paris Noir was born.[7] African-American musicians and Harlem Renaissance writers and artists in the 1920s found Paris refreshingly free of racism and open to new sights, sounds, and influences. Montmartre became the center of the small community of black American musicians, with jazz clubs such as Le Grand Duc, Chez Florence and Bricktop's thriving.

---

[7] Paris Noir and *Négritude* were allied, but not necessarily the same. If in certain quarters the Harlem Renaissance was seen as a literary and intellectual movement, *Négritude* was even more so. There tended not to be a black African or Caribbean working class in Paris at the time, and negritude catered for those blacks with aspirations to social or political leadership.

Ironically, the leaders of the Négritude movement, who engaged in their own higher view of culture, academia, and education, did not unconditionally embrace the rollicking, free-rolling jazz movement. The Harlem Renaissance writers and artists were the ones who generated more interest among blacks in Paris at the time.

Of course, this cut both ways. Through associating with so many highly accomplished black Africans, Harlem Renaissance writers and artists were exposed to African forms for the first time, and it helped them get in touch with their distant cultural roots. If the Harlem Renaissance was essentially an American experience, during which black contributors muscled into an artistic environment influenced largely by white cultural inspirations, Négritude offered a more direct line to an African heritage that had been suppressed by centuries of slavery. As Palmer Hayden noted, "I never had any desire to paint anything about Africa. I painted what Negroes, colored people, us Americans do...we're a brand new race, raised and manufactured in the US."

The Jazz Revolution

"Can it be said that America is falling prey to the collective soul of the Negro, through the influence of what is popularly known as Ragtime music? If there is any tendency to such a national disaster, it should be definitely pointed out and extreme measures taken to inhibit the influence and avert the increasing danger. Ragtime music is symbolic of the primitive morality and perceptible moral limitations of the Negro type." - *New York Herald*, 1913

By the time Hayden, Archibald Motley, Nancy Prophet, Augusta Savage, and other African-American artists were beginning to appear in Paris, the city was practically obsessed with jazz and black culture generally. In 1925, the La Revue Nègre, starring Josephine Baker accoutered in almost nothing but a large pink feather, stunned and edified Parisian audiences, beginning the career of arguably the most famous American export of the era.

If a single person should be associated with the proliferation of jazz in Paris, it would probably be Lieutenant James Reese Europe. The relatively open-armed reception of black American troops in France during World War I was aided in no small part by Senegalese Tirailleurs, who were present in large numbers in the French countryside and on the front lines. The French felt that they owed these courageous black soldiers from the colonies a great deal, and their attitude to the black presence on their shores tended to be a great deal more accommodating than the attitude back in the United States. American troops, however, brought something entirely different.

James Reese Europe was born in Mobile, Alabama in 1880, deep in the South, but his family joined the Great Migration and moved to Washington, D.C. in 1890. There, the 10 year old boy studied the violin under an assistant conductor of the United States Marine Band, after which he followed his older brother to New York. In New York, he developed a reputation as a composer and conductor, contributing to numerous theatrical productions and reviews. He also became a founding member of the influential Clef Club.

The Clef Club has been described as a musicians' hangout, fraternity club, labor exchange, and concert hall all rolled into one. The Clef Club Orchestra, created by Europe, was the first African-American orchestra in the country, numbering on average around 125 musicians and featuring a wide variety of instruments. In 1912, the Clef Club Orchestra performed on stage at Carnegie Hall, generally regarded as a seminal moment for the wider appreciation of Harlem ragtime jazz.

As in many other aspects of the Harlem Renaissance, there was a touch of elitism among black musical associations in New York and beyond, but the Clef Club made a point of accepting both "reading" musicians, trained on the violin, viola, cello, and double bass, and "non-reading" musicians who played banjos, mandolins, and harp guitars. As its reputation grew, the Clef Club achieved acceptance at the highest levels of New York's white society, and securing a genuine Clef Club Orchestra for any social event marked the height of high fashion.

In 1913, James Reese Europe became involved as musical director with the ballroom dance team of Vernon and Irene Castle. This was an interesting departure for him and the Castles, and it succeeded in raising the profile of Europe and his musicians. It also infused the Castles' dance routines with the syncopation that immediately added the missing ingredient to the modern styles that they were developing. Europe was engaged as their personal music director, with the result that he and his musicians routinely appeared in venues not traditionally friendly to black performers. As noted by author Thomas J. Hennessey, "They fueled the enormous growth of the dance hall and cabaret in this period. The social changes of urbanization brought about a significant change in the attitude towards social dancing in America, and this opened tremendous new opportunities for black jazz musicians."[8]

Europe and his Society Orchestra's association with the Castles did much to break down the general prejudice against "black music." In fact, Europe's innovative arrangement of the Memphis Blues is credited with the development of the Foxtrot.

---

[8] Hennessey, Thomas J. *From Jazz to Swing: African-American Jazz Musicians and Their Music*, 1890-1935 p 30-31.

In 1916, as the United States was nearing its entry into World War I, the 15th National Guard Regiment was formed in Harlem, comprising entirely black volunteers. James Europe signed up and was commissioned as a lieutenant, after which he was immediately ordered to organize a regimental band. Operationally, the 15th National Guard Regiment suffered the indignity of serving as a labor corps before being re-designated the 369th Regiment of the U.S. Army and attached to the French Army. Better known then as the "Harlem Hell Fighters" or the "Black Rattlers," the units saw action in several late battles on the Western Front, winning the praise of French comrades. It was the 369th's marching band, however, that won the unit more lasting recognition, not only primarily as a morale booster, but later as one of the most famous marching bands in Europe. It enlivened the somber traditions of European marching bands with lively ragtime syncopations that entirely captivated French audiences.

Europe (standing far left) with the 15th New York band

On February 9, 1919, the 369th arrived back in New York, and a week later, the regiment was honored by a parade up Fifth Avenue, and home to Harlem. Europe kept the marching band together after the unit was disbanded, and apart from a busy performance schedule, it recorded 24 instrumental and 6 vocal ensemble sides for the French recording company Pathé.

Tragically, Europe was killed in May 1919 after a knife attack during a concert at the Boston Mechanics Hall, perpetrated by one of his drummers after an argument. He died a few hours later in a Boston hospital at the age of 39. Europe received the first public funeral ever held for a black man in New York City, and band leader W. C. Handy mourned him with the following words: "The man who had just come through the baptism of war's fire and steel without a mark had been stabbed by one of his own musicians ... The sun was in the sky. The new day promised peace. But all the suns had gone down for Jim Europe, and Harlem didn't seem the same."

Europe's funeral procession

Europe may have met an untimely demise, but the seeds planted in France by his marching band of the 369th grew quickly. Several members of the band remained behind in France, and they began to organize and perform in Paris.

Others quickly followed. The district of Lower Montmartre became known as "Black Montmartre," and a vibrant culture evolved around a burgeoning culture of jazz clubs hosting numerous black American ensembles. Musically, jazz, or what was rapidly evolving into jazz, remained a fringe spectacle, popular with French audiences and well suited to the intimate venues of Lower Montmartre, but it took longer to gain acceptance as a musical form by French musicians. It was initially regarded as too American, but by the 1930s it had become more mainstream, and a long and growing list of French jazz performers and composers emerged. At one time or another, all of the African-American greats, from Louis Armstrong to Miles Davis, performed and recorded in Paris, imparting and absorbing influences and creating a cross-pollination of musical styles that benefited both.

Josephine Baker

"I have walked into the palaces of kings and queens and into the houses of presidents. And much more. But I could not walk into a hotel in America and get a cup of coffee, and that made me mad." – Josephine Baker

As part of *Shuffle Along*, Josephine Baker managed to turn a bit piece as a chorus girl into a starring role, and since she got so much attention, Sissle and Noble singled her out for special lessons and tried to add more structure and professionalism into her performances. She dutifully followed their directions in rehearsal, but once she was in front of an audience, she invariably broke out into her own wild improvisations. There was no other performer quite like her.

When *Shuffle Along* ended, Josephine was hired for Sissle and Noble's next production, in which Josephine sang and danced. *In Banville* was criticized for aspiring too much to high art and not fulfilling white audiences' expectations of black productions, but Josephine continued to get rave reviews. Despite being renamed *The Chocolate Dandies* in an effort to give it a more black spin, the show was forced to close. That said, the critical reviews suggested that Josephine met white audiences' expectations of black comics.

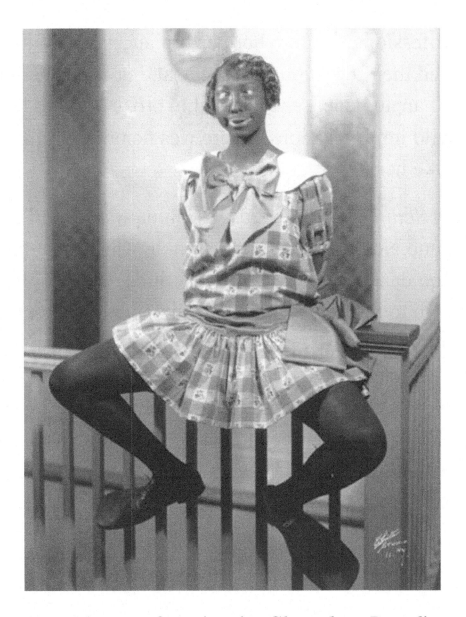

Josephine performing in *Chocolate Dandies*

In the wake of the show ending, a number of the cast members were moving to Harlem, and Josephine went with them. It was 1924 and the Harlem Renaissance was in full swing. She was soon hired in the revue *Tan Town Topics,* which was playing at the Plantation Theater Restaurant, and she was well-established enough by now to get her own featured billing as "the highest paid chorus girl in vaudeville." The shows at the Plantation Theater Restaurant started at midnight and attracted white after-theater goers; well-to-do blacks were allowed but had to sit at corner tables. Even in Harlem, even at the height of its Renaissance, segregation prevailed. Ethel Waters was singing in the show at the time, but one night she had laryngitis and Josephine took her place. She was afraid at first, but characteristically she rose to the occasion and was met with a standing ovation.

Josephine was never one to rest on the successes she racked up, and in 1925, she was offered a chance to perform in France, by Carolyn Dudley, a rich American woman, who planned to bring a troupe of black dancers and singers to Paris. Paris had become crazy for the American "jazz-age", which the American forces had brought with them during World War I, and a number of black musicians who had served in the forces stayed in Paris, sensing that it was more liberal and less racist. Josephine would later echo this sentiment: "I wanted to get far away from those who believed in cruelty, so then I went to France, a land of true freedom, democracy, equality and fraternity."

Josephine set sail for France in 1925 at the age of 19, and like the performers who stayed in France after World War I, one of the main reasons Josephine decided to go to France was her increasing hatred of the racism in

America. Josephine realized that no matter how successful a performer she became, she would still be treated as a second-class citizen, even in New York. As Josephine stood at the rail of the steamship leaving for Paris, her life passed before her in review. She later wrote, "When the Statute of Liberty disappeared over the horizon, I knew that I was free."

The steamship docked at Le Havre a week later, and Josephine boarded the train for Paris. She and the other black members of the troupe headed for the club car to get coffee and croissants, and they were welcomed with smiles, their first experience of true integration. At the Paris train station, Josephine and the rest of the troupe boarded a bus for the Theater des Champs-Elysees, where their show was to play. Waiting outside the theater for them was the up-and-coming artist Paul Colin, who had been commissioned to illustrate the poster advertising *La Negre Revue*, as their show had been named. Paul Colin had only 24 hours to illustrate the poster, and during the rehearsals, Colin was much more taken with Josephine and her specialty dance than the show's billed star, Maude de Forrest. Through an interpreter, he asked her to come to his studio that night, where he convinced her to strip down to her slip while striking dance poses as he made numerous sketches of her. Josephine later said it was the first time she felt truly beautiful, and the poster featuring

Josephine became quite famous in its own right.

Colin's poster

Meanwhile, the director of the theater, Andre Davan, was unhappy with the way Carol Dudley had put the show together. He hired choreographer Jacques Charles, who, after watching a run-through, immediately wanted to feature Josephine more prominently. He and Davan both wanted her to do her version of the Charleston, which as all the rage in America at the time, but Charles also thought that what was missing for Parisian audiences was the erotic, especially the primal, exotic, wild version of erotic they projected onto Africans and African-Americans. Thus, Charles created a "danse sauvage" for her to be performed with a black dancer, Joe Alex, originally from the West Indies, who played in a Montmartre club, and both performers were to be dressed only in skirts of feathers as Charles conceptualized "true Africans."

Josephine in the show in 1925

Josephine and Joe Alex

Charles' ideas meant that Josephine would have to appear topless, which was common among dance hall performers and chorus girls in Paris, but not so much with stars of shows, and legitimate American performers did not appear with bare breasts. Moreover, while the French projected their stereotypes of "African primitives" on African-Americans, Josephine's African-American cultural roots were something quite different, and the French choreographer's imagined sexualized African dance was not familiar to Josephine at all. African-American dancing bore resemblances to African dance, flat-footed with different rhythms in different parts of the body at the same time, but Charles' imagined danse sauvage was not even an authentic African dance. Josephine did not want to appear half-naked, nor do a "primitive" dance. Having thought Paris would offer her a higher artistic platform, she now began to have misgivings.

Fortunately, Josephine's fears were quelled quickly on opening night when her first number, a comic Charleston, was met with enthusiastic audience approval. When it came time for her to do the dance sauvage at the end of the show, by her own admission, a kind of ecstasy possessed her as she did the seductive, wildly rhythmic dance. As she later wrote, "Driven by dark forces I didn't recognize, I improvised, crazed by the music, the overheated theater filled to the bursting point, the scorching eye of the spotlights…Each time I leaped I seemed to touch the sky and when I returned to earth it seemed to be mine alone." At the end of the dance, the crowd jumped to their feet applauding passionately, and some even rushed the stage. The critics called her "African Eros" and "the black Venus," while Picasso himself termed her "the Nefertiti of now". There was a huge rush on tickets for the show, and journalists swarmed outside Josephine's hotel room the next morning. Josephine Baker had become a Parisian star in one night.

As the *Negre Revue* enjoyed increasing success, Josephine was lavished with gifts from fans, including fancy ball gowns and jewelry. She lived in a 2 bedroom suite in the Hotel Fournet. She bought herself a collection of dolls, something she had wanted since she was a child, and named each one. She also kept a small menagerie of animals in her suite, including two rabbits, a parakeet, a snake, and a pig named Albert. Josephine later said she told the animals everything, both her joys and her hurts.

Moreover, Carolyn Dudley introduced Josephine to the famous French clothes designer Paul Poiret who began to design couture for her. Josephine's dress became quite chic to the further delight of the Parisians. Josephine became lovers with Paul Colin, the artist who had featured her on the posters for the revue. He introduced her to Parisian society and artists, in particular, started clamoring for her attention, wanting to paint and sculpt her. Josephine's image was also on postcards on stalls throughout the city. Josephine Baker had become the toast of Paris at only 19 years old. She later remarked, "Paris is the dance, I am the dancer."

Theater des Champs Elysees played theatrical shows, including those avant-garde and those that mixed high and low brow (as was the rage at that time), but Folies Bergere was the oldest and fanciest of Paris dance halls. Indeed, the women did wear feathers, which was the root of Caroline Dudley's comment about turning Josephine into a "trussed-up mannequin". Although the Folies Bergere had been founded in 1896, it was not until 1907 that the first nudity appeared, and for a while, it took on a reputation for debauchery, full of prostitution.

However, when Derval took over the Folies Bergere in 1919, he cleaned it up considerably and made it more palatable to the bourgeoisie and respectable society. He ran the prostitutes who congregated around the building out and changed the nudity of the dance hall girls from primarily "erotic" to primarily "aesthetic". Maurice Chevalier, Edith Piaf, and Mistinguett, the French chanteuse, had all played the stage, and each show was programmed around a theme, so Derval chose "primitive vitality" for the theme of Folies du Jour with Josephine Baker. The primitive vitality of her dancing was to be showcased against scenes portraying the frippery of civilization, from Louis XIV's mistresses to window shopping Parisian flappers who did a humorous "striptease" by putting on clothes over half-naked bodies rather than removing them.

By the time the show started, over half a million dollars went into staging the production. Erte, one of the most notable Art Deco artists, worked on the set design,

Josephine's name was up in lights at the theater, and color photographs advertised her performances. There was one number in which Josephine was lowered to the ground in a huge glittering, golden cage shaped like an egg, and when the door unhinged, it revealed Josephine dancing the Charleston on a mirror, with the image of her nearly naked body reflecting off a number of other mirrored surfaces in the theater and virtually turning her into a piece of living cubist artwork.

Josephine did another number, the Banana Dance, which was to become her signature dance. Some critics may believe that Josephine did become a trussed up dance hall queen whose image became more commodified at the expense of her art and uniqueness, but Josephine believed her body was her work of art, and she was fine with the show. As she once put it, "A violinist had a violin, a painter his palette. All I had was myself. I was the instrument that I must care for."

Pictures of Josephine in the famous banana costume

All the while, Josephine's popularity continued to soar. By the end of 1926, she was thought to be the most photographed woman in the world, and it was rumored she had received over 40,000 love letters and 2000 marriage proposals. Josephine Baker dolls sold by the thousands, and her image was featured in advertising.

Josephine even found herself in the unexpected position of being held up by white women as a template of beauty; her celebrity brought on new momentum for suntans started by Chanel and the Riviera high-society set, while creams and hair pomades featuring her name were introduced. To young women, she was a symbol of liberation as the Charleston dancing flapper, or la garconne as it was called in France.

During the late stages of the decade, Josephine remained atop the pinnacle of Parisian society. Picasso painted her, Alexander Calder sculpted her into one of his famous mobiles, F. Scott Fitzgerald referred to her "chocolate arabesques'" in *Babylon Revisited*, and Ernest Hemingway claimed he danced the night away with her while she wore a fur coat with nothing underneath. At one point, Josephine was gifted with a Voisin automobile painted brown to match the color of her skin and upholstered in snakeskin.

Eventually, Josephine moved out of Montmartre with its easygoing ethnic mix to an apartment in a more upscale neighborhood. The sophisticates of high Parisian society still wined and dined Josephine, but she was often painfully aware of how hard it was for her to keep up, and in spite of all the adulation, ugly racism still cropped up. Although *Vogue* magazine proclaimed "the Negro composes better than Beethoven…dances better than

Nijinsky", the city's leading cartoonist, Sem, caricatured Josephine as a monkey in an evening dress with a tail swatting a fly. Ironically, while white women tanned their skin to become more like Josephine, Josephine often rubbed herself with lemon juice and bathed in goat's milk and bleach, although it was painful, to become lighter. Many French men wanted to be her lover, but at the mention of marriage and children, they recoiled. All of this drove home the fact that even if the Parisian bourgeoisie loved the dance halls, they did not consider its performers "respectable."

During parts of 1931-1932, Josephine toured Europe, returning to the Casino de Paris for a show called La Joie de Paris. In some numbers, she fused the jerky and angular movements of vernacular black dancing with ballet. There was also a strange number that made fun of the sun tanning fad by pointing out that these women were now lighter skinned than Josephine. It is interesting that Paris was described as non-racist, but still these odd ways of using Josephine's race as a source of humor is a form of racism, even if more subtle. In 1933 Josephine went on a world tour that even briefly included parts of Asia and Africa.

A promotional shot of Josephine for La Joie de Paris

In 1935, Josephine was booked with the Ziegfried Follies in a show that was to include Fanny Brice and Bob Hope, with musical numbers by Ira Gershwin. Josephine Baker would be the first black woman to appear in the Ziegfried Follies, and, as it turned out, she was also the last. She sailed to New York, and as she passed the Statute of Liberty coming into New York, Josephine remembered passing it on the way out of New York all those years before. She thought about how much she had changed, and how much confidence she had gained. Ironically, she probably should have remembered her thoughts upon leaving about finally being free because she soon found out she still was a second-class citizen in New York. Greeted at the port by large numbers of the press, she took a cab to her hotel, the St. Moritz, only to have the manager check her in and tell her that she must never enter through the lobby again.

She faced more vitriolic racism in some of the criticisms of her performance in the show, especially the following in *Time* magazine: "Josephine Baker is a washer-woman's daughter who stepped out of a Negro burlesque show into a life of adulation and luxury in Paris during the booming 1920s. In sex appeal to jaded Europeans of the jazz-loving type, a Negro wench has a head start…But to Manhattan theatre-goers last week she was just a slightly buck-toothed young Negro woman whose figure might be matched in any night club show, and whose dancing and singing might be topped anywhere outside of Paris." Along with the racism, the comment also assumed an air of cultural superiority over France.

Many African-Americans also continued to criticize her,

finding her too European and not identifying with her performances. Upon hearing that she was barred from certain hotels and clubs, some even went so far as to say she deserved it. However, one black journalist, Roi Ottley, championed her and wrote in a Harlem newspaper, "Harlem, instead of taking up the cudgel of prejudiced whites, should rally to the side of this courageous Negro woman. We should make her insults our insults." Ironically, Josephine once disguised herself and sang a song at Harlem's Apollo Theater under the name "Gracie Walker". The Apollo was notorious for being rough on performers, booing many of the acts off the stage, but "Gracie King" got through her number uninterrupted. It should also be noted that the white audiences at the Ziegfried Follies seemed to like Josephine's performances more than the critics.

Josephine arrived back in Paris on June 2, 1936, a day before her 30th birthday. She was greeted by a number of fans carrying bouquets, and a newsreel camera man with an accordion player who coaxed her into singing "J'ai Deux Amours". After her experiences in Europe, Josephine might have had a greater love for Paris than her country of birth. At the same time, she was somewhat lonely; she longed to be married and have children, but despite the fact the French were less racist than Americans and more than willing to carry on affairs with her, they were not willing to marry her, often due to family opinion on the matter of marrying a black woman (especially one who was a "dance hall performer").

During World War II, Josephine was active in the Red Cross, working also with the Free French and the French Resistance, winning for her courage the Croix de Guerre and the Legion of Honour with the rosette of the Resistance, two of France's highest military honors. In later life she was active in the Civil Rights movement, participating in demonstrations and refusing to perform at segregated clubs and concert venues. In 1963, she participated alongside Martin Luther King in the March on Washington, and she was among many eminent speakers at the event.

In 1973, after years of being ostracized by mainstream American audiences, she performed at Carnegie Hall to a standing ovation, marking a return to public performance, but on April 12, 1975, she died in her sleep of a cerebral haemorrhage at age 68. She was buried in Paris with full military honors.

Josephine Baker loved fairy tales, and in many ways, her life reads like one as she persevered through a childhood in the slums of St. Louis to become one of Paris' most glamorous and beloved performers. But it was not a prince on a white horse or a fairy godmother who made her dreams come true; instead, it was Josephine's sheer determination, talent, charisma, and unique style of performing that gave rise to her stardom. All along the way, she fought against racism, whether it was joining the French Resistance to fight against the Nazis or working with the NAACP to fight racial segregation in America. Through everything, she kept performing, entertaining people all over the globe with her dancing and singing, and she left a lasting influence on the movement.

Conclusion

"If the American Negro is to have a culture of his own he will have to leave America to get it." – Paul Robeson

One overarching irony of the Harlem Renaissance and the New Negro Movement was that the people involved depended in many ways on white audiences, white art collectors, white literary critics, and white publishers. The stratification of society through centuries of slavery and racism meant that few blacks had the economic resources to support a full-scale cultural emergence of this sort. Moreover, famous black performers who found acceptance among white audiences ended up playing venues that black customers themselves could not attend. This had the effect, in the opinion of a great many subsequent analysts and historians, of turning Harlem into an enlarged stage performance that was financially dependent on white patronage. In turn, as the 1920s progressed, black artists and writers began increasingly to resent this reliance on white economic support and the attitudes of patronization that inevitably followed.

As a result, while the explosion of creativity and production that characterized the New Negro Movement helped establish a crossover of black styles of expression to white audiences, it also required a degree of cultural assimilation that leaned more heavily on blacks compromising than whites. The "New Negro," many remarked, existed as nothing more than a secondary reflection of white standards of dress, manners, etiquette, and artistic expressions, in particular among the higher forms of literary and artistic experimentation. As such, critics claimed, the movement offered little that was unique or original.

There are others, however, bearing in mind the tenor of the times, who see this as a major accomplishment within itself. It was inevitable that a subjugated minority would have little choice other than to begin such a cultural transition in a state of dependency. In that light, the ability to open the doors to white publishing houses, galleries, theaters, newspapers, and periodicals should be seen as a major achievement. In the same vein, many prominent black figures like Du Bois still saw significant value in classical European themes, and they aimed to see blacks replicate those themes.

Ultimately, the Harlem Renaissance and the New Negro Movement began the process that would culminate with the Civil Rights Movement and the ongoing struggle that continues to this day. To establish a separate identity – separate not only from the dominant forces in society, but also from the long forgotten traditions of a life lost in a distant past – surely marked the genesis of a people embarking on a long journey of self-discovery. Artistically, African-American writers and artists began influencing one another and increasingly drawing influences from Africa, but they also began to influence whites. Thousands of whites came to Harlem to experience the nightlife, and inevitably, white composers, dramatists, and writers began to utilize the creative tendencies and themes of African-Americans in their own works. As a result, the Harlem Renaissance was the very much a coming of age for black people in America, and as Du Bois himself aptly asserted, "The Talented Tenth of the Negro race must be made leaders of thought and missionaries of culture among their people."

Online Resources

Other 20th century history titles by Charles River Editors

Other titles about the Harlem Renaissance on Amazon

Further Reading

Amos, Shawn, compiler. *Rhapsodies in Black: Words and Music of the Harlem Renaissance*. Los Angeles: Rhino Records, 2000. 4 Compact Discs.

Andrews, William L.; Frances S. Foster; Trudier Harris, eds. *The Concise Oxford Companion To African American Literature*. New York: Oxford Press, 2001. ISBN 1-4028-9296-9

Bean, Annemarie. *A Sourcebook on African-American Performance: Plays, People, Movements*. London: Routledge, 1999; pp. vii + 360.

Greaves, William documentary *From These Roots*.

Hicklin, Fannie Ella Frazier. 'The American Negro Playwright, 1920–1964.' Ph.D. Dissertation, Department of Speech, University of Wisconsin, 1965. Ann Arbor: University Microfilms 65-6217.

Huggins, Nathan. *Harlem Renaissance*. New York: Oxford University Press, 1973. ISBN 0-19-501665-3

Hughes, Langston. *The Big Sea*. New York: Knopf, 1940.

Hutchinson, George. *The Harlem Renaissance in Black and White*. New York: Belknap Press, 1997. ISBN 0-674-37263-8

King, Shannon. *Whose Harlem Is This, Anyway? Community Politics and Grassroots Activism during the New Negro Era*. New York: New York University Press, 2015.

Lewis, David Levering, ed. *The Portable Harlem Renaissance Reader*. New York: Viking Penguin, 1995. ISBN 0-14-017036-7

Lewis, David Levering. *When Harlem Was in Vogue*. New York: Penguin, 1997. ISBN 0-14-026334-9

Ostrom, Hans. *A Langston Hughes Encyclopedia*. Westport: Greenwood Press, 2002.

Ostrom, Hans and J. David Macey, eds. *The Greenwood Encylclopedia of African American Literature*. 5 volumes. Westport: Greenwood Press, 2005.

Padva, Gilad. "Black Nostalgia: Poetry, Ethnicity, and Homoeroticism in *Looking for Langston* and *Brother to Brother*". In Padva, Gilad, *Queer Nostalgia in Cinema and Pop Culture*, pp. 199–226. Basingstock, UK, and New York: Palgrave Macmillan, 2014.

Patton, Venetria K. and Maureen Honey, eds. *Double-Take: A Revisionist Harlem Renaissance Anthology.* New Jersey: Rutgers University Press, 2006.

Perry, Jeffrey B. *A Hubert Harrison Reader.* Middletown, CT: Wesleyan University Press, 2001.

Perry, Jeffrey B. *Hubert Harrison: The Voice of Harlem Radicalism, 1883–1918.* New York: Columbia University Press, 2008.

Powell, Richard, and David A. Bailey, eds. *Rhapsodies in Black: Art of the Harlem Renaissance.* Berkeley: University of California Press, 1997.

Rampersad, Arnold. *The Life of Langston Hughes.* 2 volumes. New York: Oxford University Press, 1986 and 1988.

Robertson, Stephen, et al., "Disorderly Houses: Residences, Privacy, and the Surveillance of Sexuality in 1920s Harlem," *Journal of the History of Sexuality,* 21 (September 2012), 443–66.

Soto, Michael, ed. *Teaching The Harlem Renaissance.* New York: Peter Lang, 2008.

Tracy, Steven C. *Langston Hughes and the Blues.* Urbana: University of Illinois Press, 1988.

Watson, Steven. *The Harlem Renaissance: Hub of African-American Culture, 1920–1930.* New York: Pantheon Books, 1995. ISBN 0-679-75889-5

Williams, Iain Cameron. "Underneath a Harlem Moon ... The Harlem to Paris Years of Adelaide Hall". Continuum Int. Publishing, 2003. ISBN 0826458939

Wintz, Cary D. *Black Culture and the Harlem Renaissance.* Houston: Rice University Press, 1988.

Wintz, Cary D. *Harlem Speaks: A Living History of the Harlem Renaissance.* Naperville, Illinois: Sourcebooks, Inc., 2007

Free Books by Charles River Editors

We have brand new titles available for free most days of the week. To see which of our titles are currently free, click on this link.

Discounted Books by Charles River Editors

We have titles at a discount price of just 99 cents everyday. To see which of our titles are currently 99 cents, click on this link.

Made in the USA
Las Vegas, NV
25 March 2022